ROUTE 66 CENTENNIAL

Pack your car and fill the tank. Adventure—and plenty of neon—awaits on the Mother Road.

Can you hear it? Like the throaty rumble of a V-8 engine, the open road is calling for you to fill up the tank and put on your favorite playlist. As Route 66 gets set to celebrate its centennial this year, there's no better time to experience its varied landscapes, neon signs, roadside motels, mom-and-pop shops, family-owned diners, quirky attractions, and small-town hospitality.

Officially established on November 11, 1926, US Route 66 was stitched together from nearly 2,448 miles of local, state, and federal roads that connected Chicago to Santa Monica, California. Signage didn't appear until the following year, and it took until 1938 for the entire eight-state route to be fully paved. Still, one hundred years ago, Route 66 began to beckon entrepreneurs, travelers, and those seeking something more.

With 507 miles in 1926, New Mexico contained the longest stretch of any state. A realignment in 1937 shaved off more than 100 miles across the state, but it also added to the Mother Road's mystique. The route has since become more than a way to get from Illinois to California. Across the U.S., it connects history, scenery, and culture.

That's what we tried to capture in this commemorative calendar, featuring some of our favorite sights in Tucumcari, Santa Rosa, Albuquerque, Santa Fe, Grants, and Gallup. Hopefully, you'll find the inspiration to pack up the car, hit the road, and make memories of your own.

—Steve Gleydura, Editor in Chief, *New Mexico Magazine*

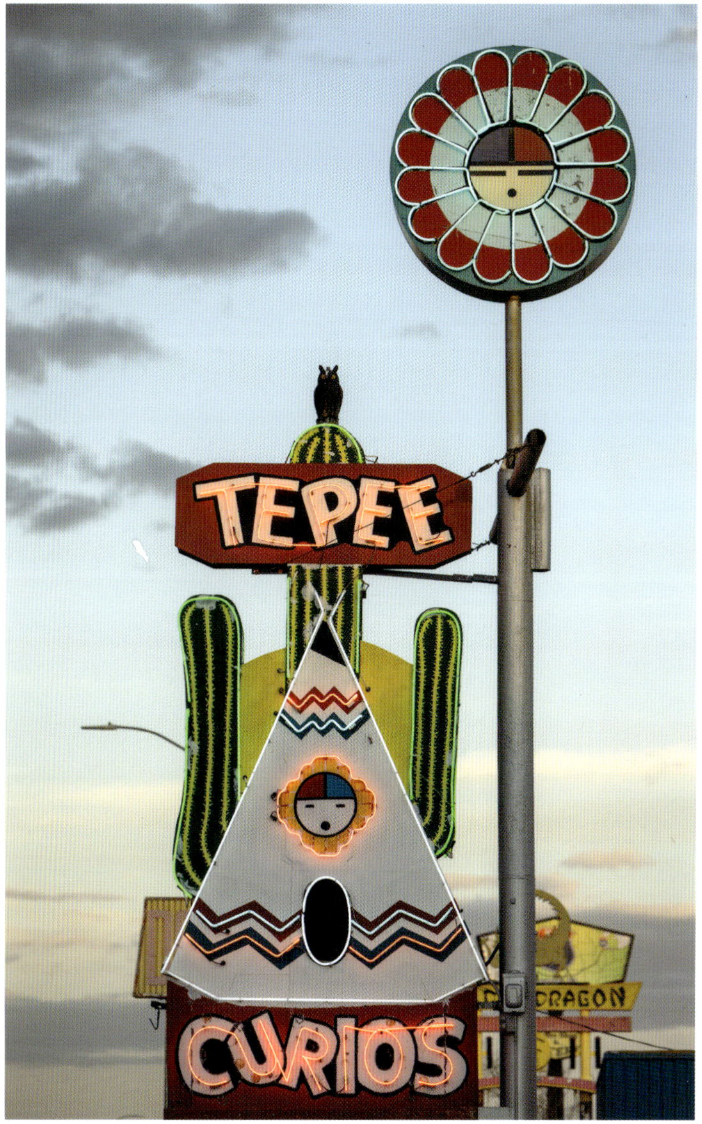

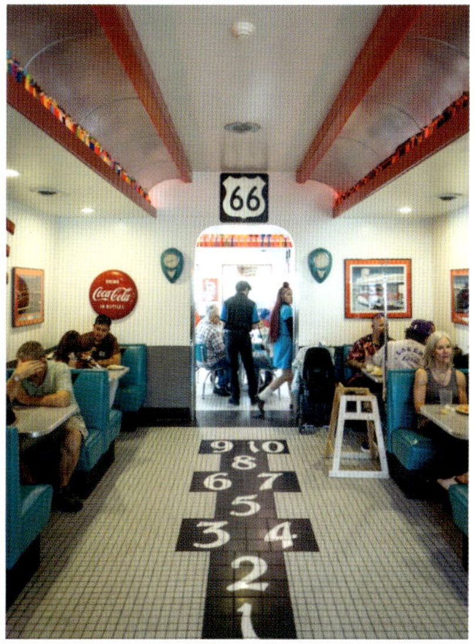

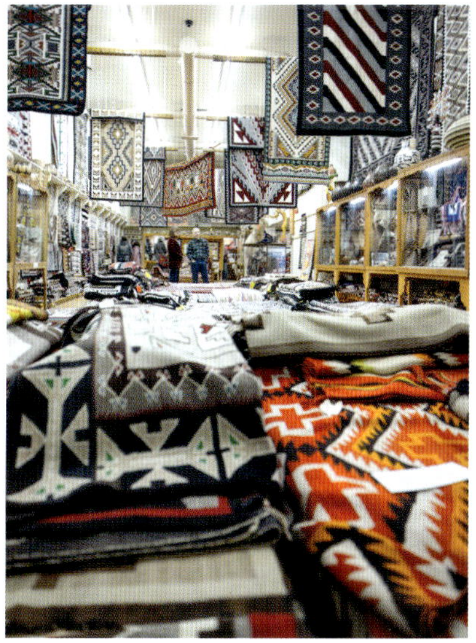

Front cover: Albuquerque's Central Avenue shines at night. **Previous page:** The Trade Station Gift Shop in Tucumcari has been restored to look like a vintage Texaco station. **This page, clockwise from left:** TeePee Curios, in Tucumcari. Albuquerque's 66 Diner. The rug room at Richardson Trading Post in Gallup. All photographs by Jen Judge.

AF731467

NEW MEXICO, USA
ROUTE 66 CENTENNIAL
1926-2026
LAND OF ENCHANTMENT

New Mexico
MAGAZINE

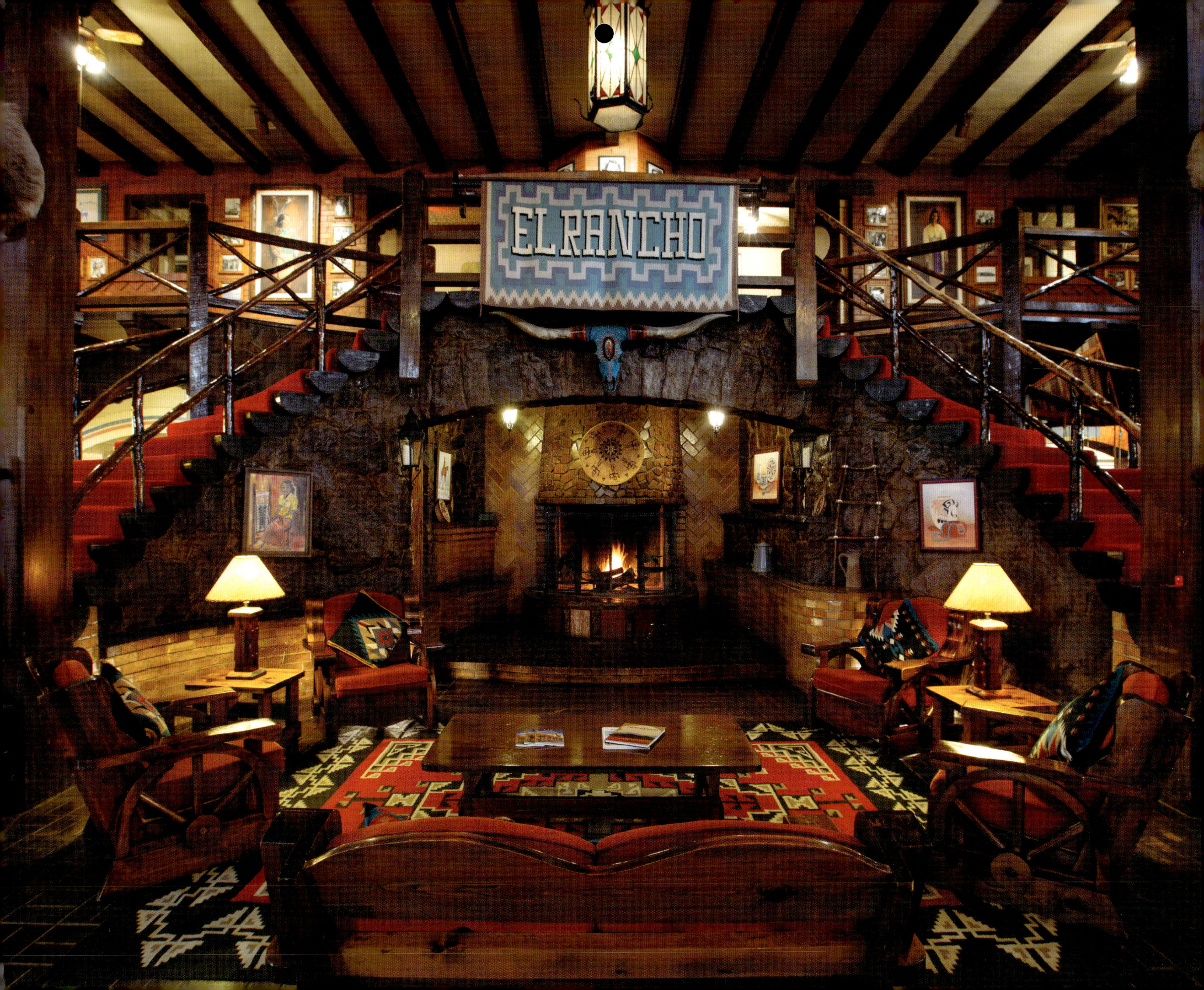
EL RANCHO

DECEMBER 2025						
	1	2	3	4	5	6
7	8	9	10	11	12	13
14	15	16	17	18	19	20
21	22	23	24	25	26	27
28	29	30	31			

January 2026

FEBRUARY 2026						
1	2	3	4	5	6	7
8	9	10	11	12	13	14
15	16	17	18	19	20	21
22	23	24	25	26	27	28

SUNDAY	MONDAY	TUESDAY	WEDNESDAY	THURSDAY	FRIDAY	SATURDAY
				1 New Year's Day	2	3 Full Moon
4	5	6	7	8	9	10
11	12	13	14	15	16	17
18	19 Martin Luther King Jr. Day	20	21	22	23 San Ildefonso Pueblo Feast Day	24
25	26	27	28	29	30	31

Step into the Old West at the El Rancho Hotel in Gallup.
Photograph by Kate Russell.

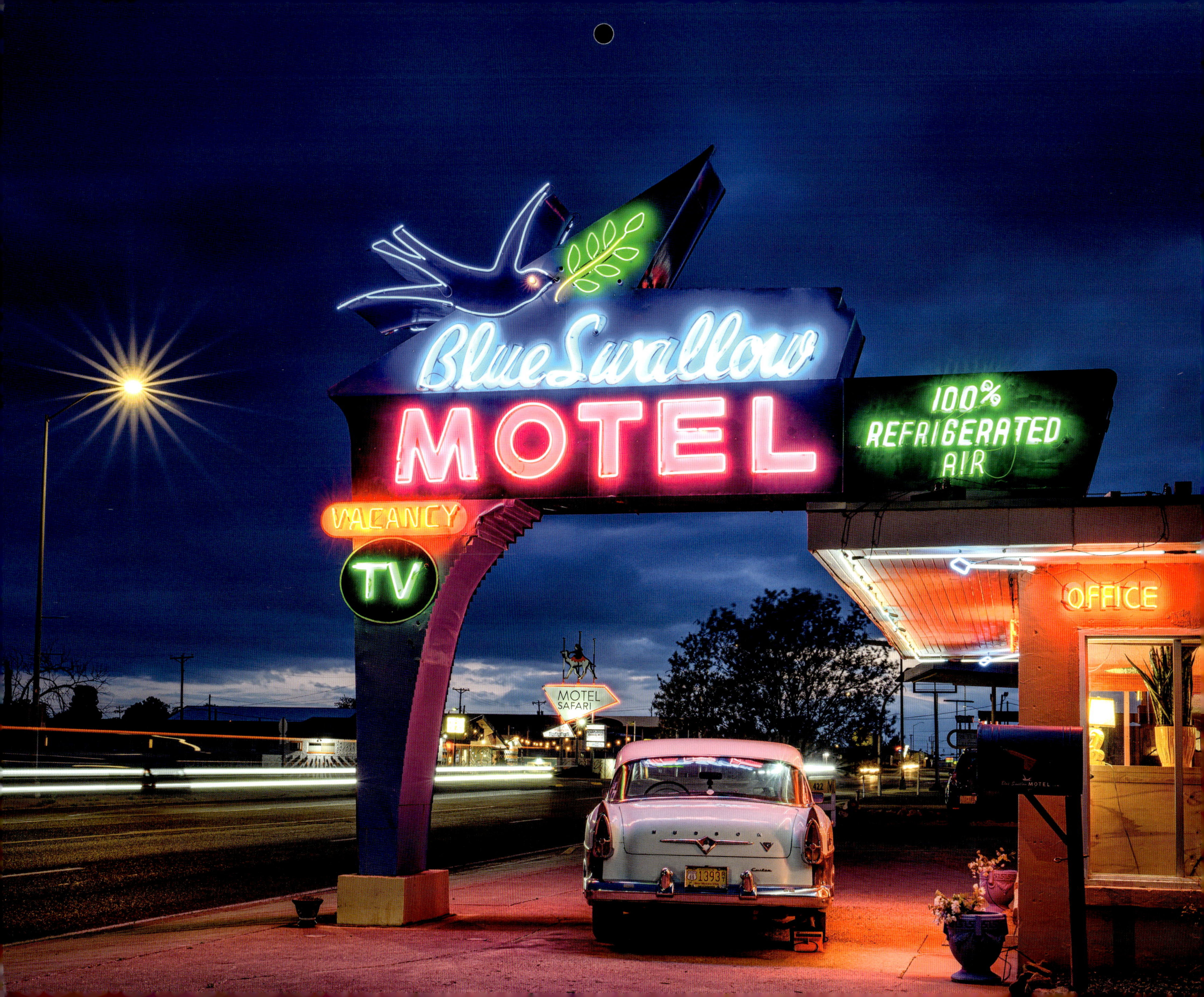
Blue Swallow
MOTEL
100%
REFRIGERATED
AIR
VACANCY
TV
OFFICE
MOTEL
SAFARI

JANUARY 2026

				1	2	3
4	5	6	7	8	9	10
11	12	13	14	15	16	17
18	19	20	21	22	23	24
25	26	27	28	29	30	31

February 2026

MARCH 2026

1	2	3	4	5	6	7
8	9	10	11	12	13	14
15	16	17	18	19	20	21
22	23	24	25	26	27	28
29	30	31				

SUNDAY	MONDAY	TUESDAY	WEDNESDAY	THURSDAY	FRIDAY	SATURDAY
1 First day of Black History Month ○ Full Moon	2 Groundhog Day	3	4	5	6	7
8	9	10	11	12	13	14 Valentine's Day
15	16 Presidents' Day	17	18	19	20	21
22	23	24	25	26	27	28

The iconic neon sign welcomes travelers to the Blue Swallow Motel in Tucumcari.
Photograph by Reece Parker.

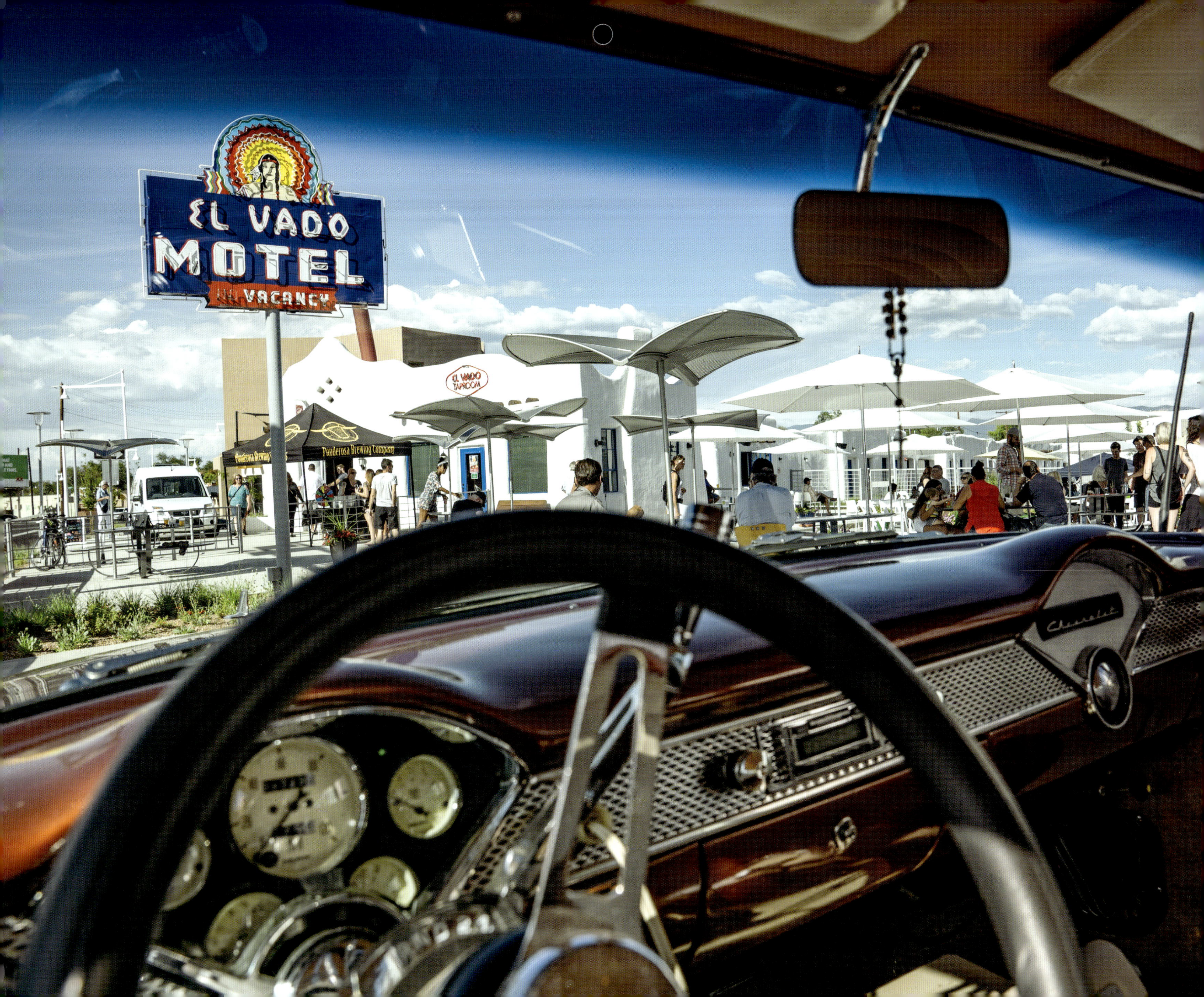
EL VADO
MOTEL
VACANCY
EL VADO TAPROOM
Ponderosa Brewing Company
Chevrolet

FEBRUARY 2026						
1	2	3	4	5	6	7
8	9	10	11	12	13	14
15	16	17	18	19	20	21
22	23	24	25	26	27	28

March 2026

APRIL 2026						
			1	2	3	4
5	6	7	8	9	10	11
12	13	14	15	16	17	18
19	20	21	22	23	24	25
26	27	28	29	30		

SUNDAY	MONDAY	TUESDAY	WEDNESDAY	THURSDAY	FRIDAY	SATURDAY
1 First day of Women's History Month	2	3 Full Moon	4	5	6	7
8	9	10	11	12	13	14
15	16	17 St. Patrick's Day	18	19 Laguna Pueblo Feast Day	20	21
22	23	24	25	26	27	28
29	30	31				

With its food court, the El Vado Motel in Albuquerque is more than a spot to spend the night.
Photograph by Jakob Schiller.

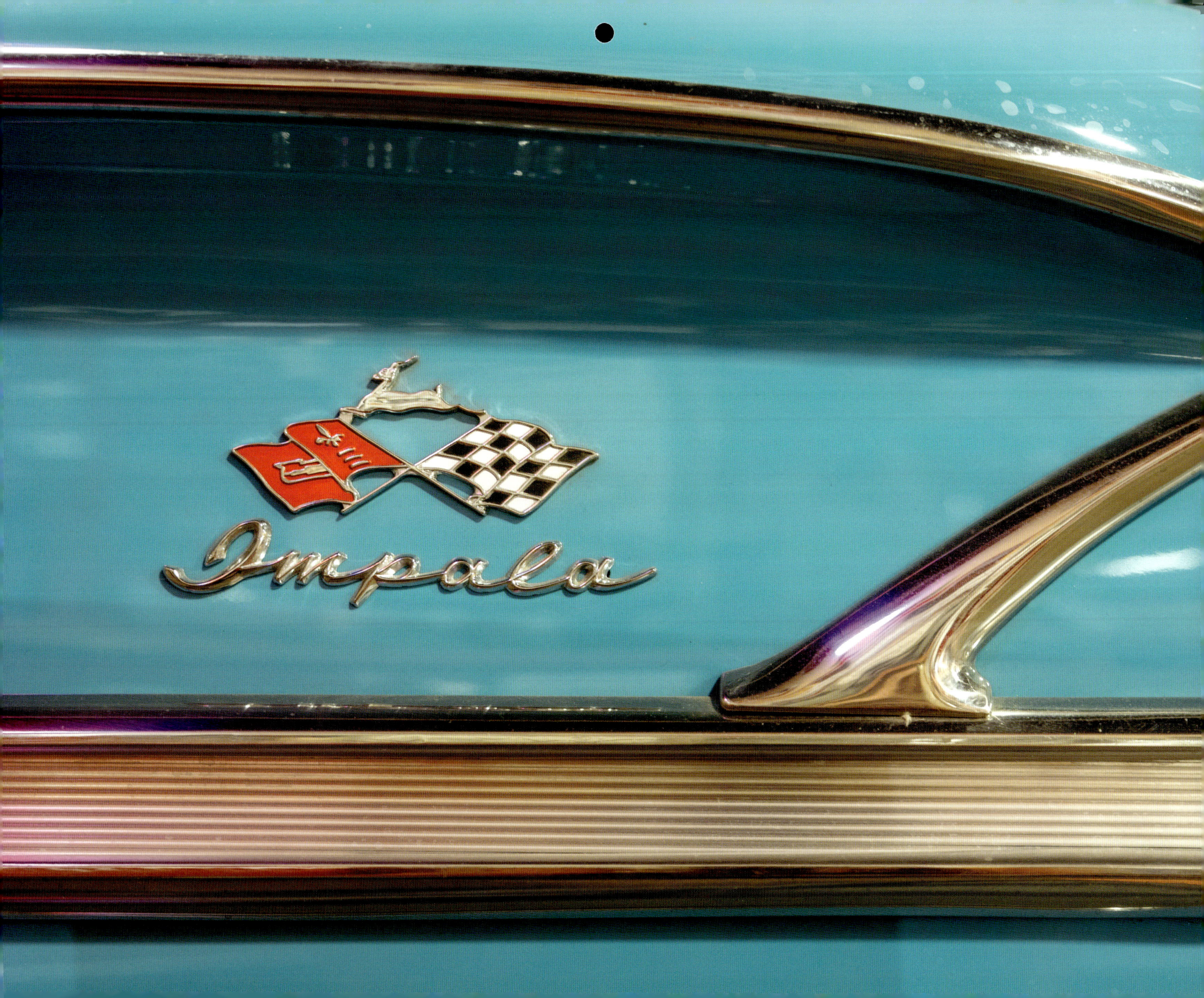
Impala

April 2026

MARCH 2026

1	2	3	4	5	6	7
8	9	10	11	12	13	14
15	16	17	18	19	20	21
22	23	24	25	26	27	28
29	30	31				

MAY 2026

					1	2
3	4	5	6	7	8	9
10	11	12	13	14	15	16
17	18	19	20	21	22	23
24/31	25	26	27	28	29	30

SUNDAY	MONDAY	TUESDAY	WEDNESDAY	THURSDAY	FRIDAY	SATURDAY
			1 Beginning of Passover Full Moon	2	3 Good Friday	4
5 Easter	6 Easter Monday	7	8	9	10	11
12	13	14	15 Tax Day	16	17	18
19	20	21	22 Earth Day	23	24	25
26	27	28	29	30		

The Route 66 Auto Museum in Santa Rosa features more than 30 hot rods, vintage automobiles, and classic cars.
Photograph by Jen Judge.

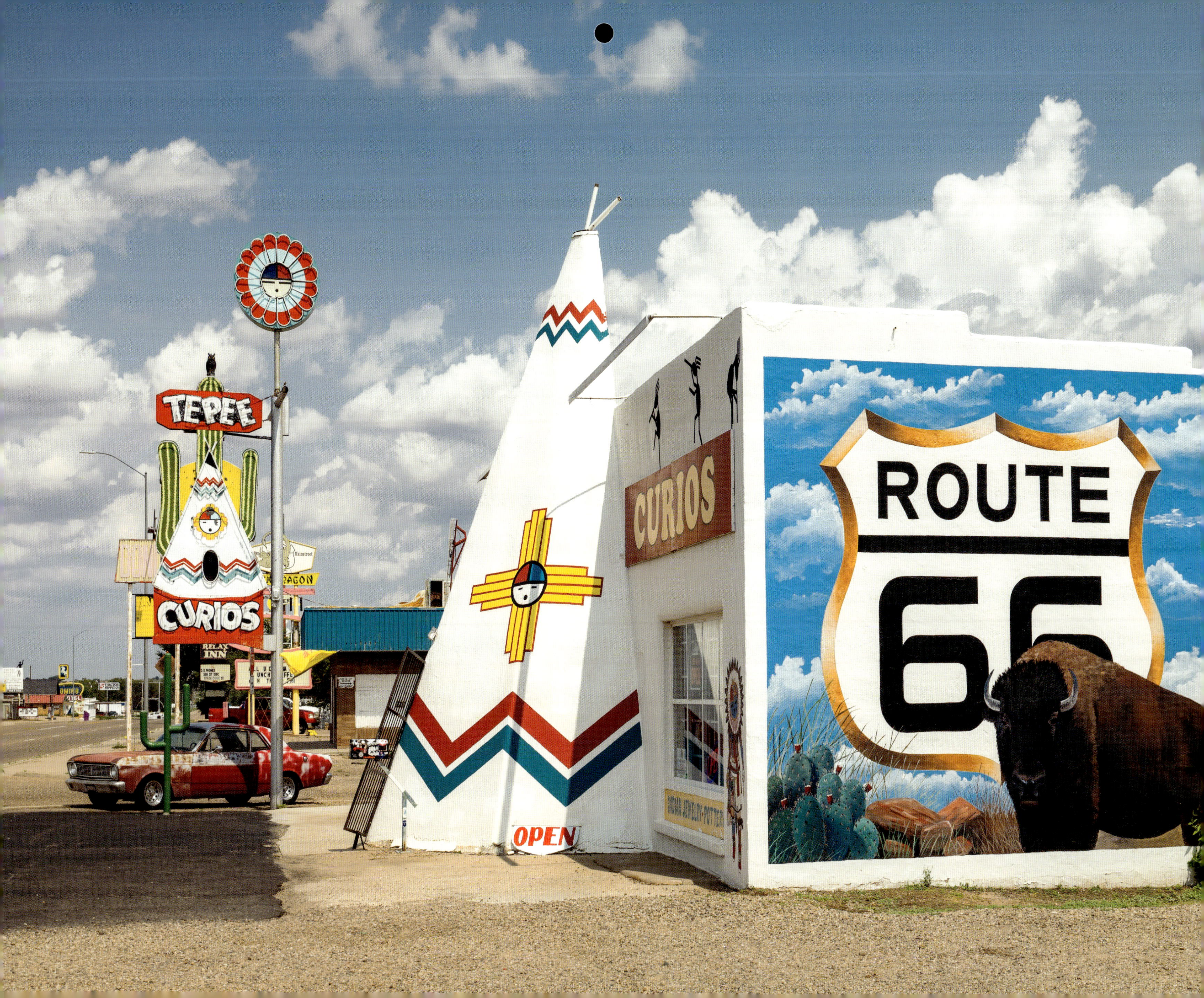
TEPEE
CURIOS
CURIOS
ROUTE
66
OPEN
RELAX INN

May 2026

APRIL 2026

			1	2	3	4
5	6	7	8	9	10	11
12	13	14	15	16	17	18
19	20	21	22	23	24	25
26	27	28	29	30		

JUNE 2026

	1	2	3	4	5	6
7	8	9	10	11	12	13
14	15	16	17	18	19	20
21	22	23	24	25	26	27
28	29	30				

SUNDAY	MONDAY	TUESDAY	WEDNESDAY	THURSDAY	FRIDAY	SATURDAY
					1 First day of Asian American and Pacific Islander Heritage Month San Felipe Pueblo Feast Day Full Moon	2
3 Acoma Pueblo Feast Day Taos Pueblo Feast Day	4	5	6	7	8	9
10 Mother's Day	11	12	13	14	15	16
17	18	19	20	21	22	23
24 / 31 Full Moon	25 Memorial Day	26	27	28	29	30

Check out the buffalo mural and souvenirs at TeePee Curios in Tucumcari.
Photograph by Gabriella Marks.

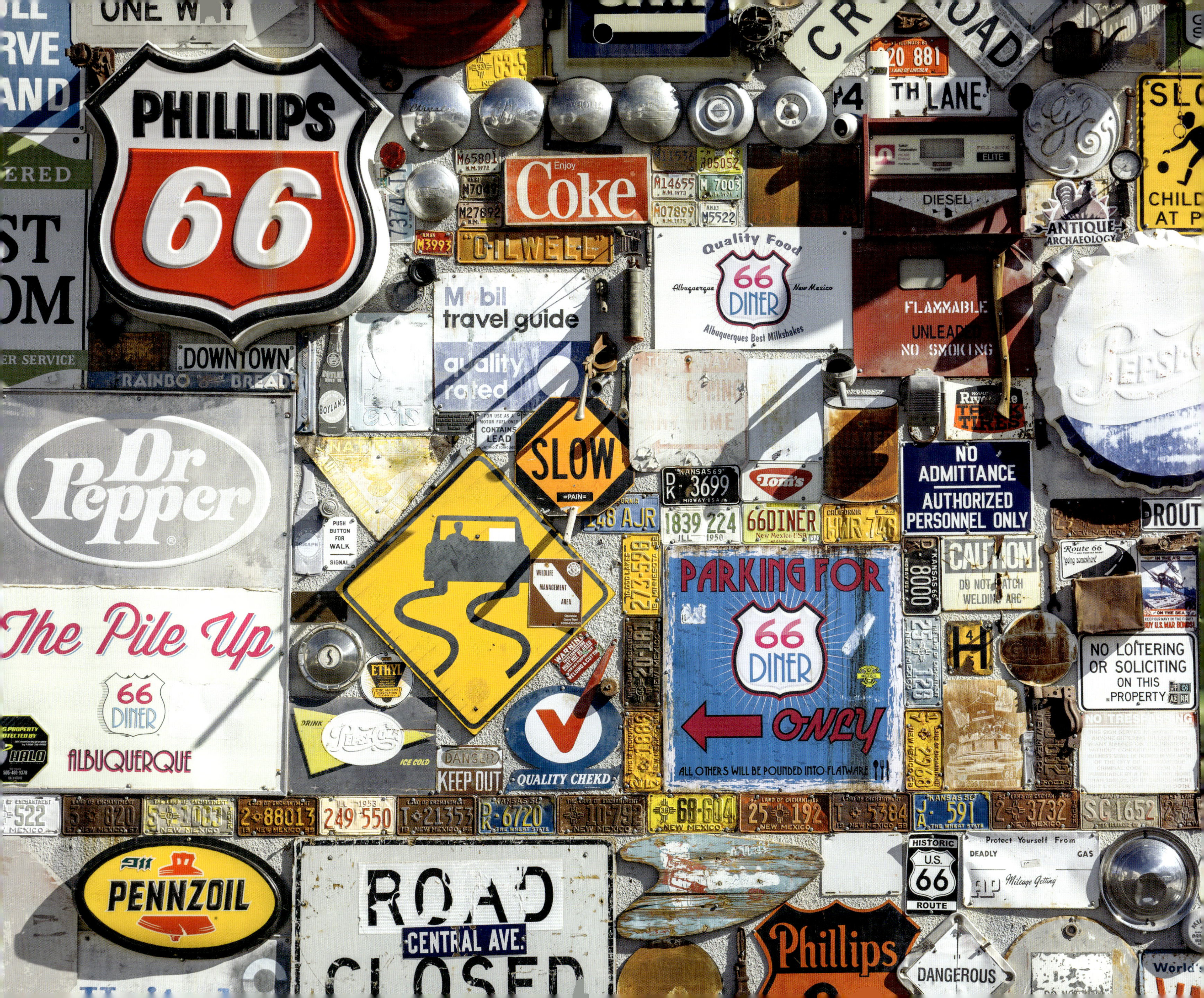
PHILLIPS 66
Coke
Enjoy
OILWELL
Quality Food
66 DINER
Albuquerque New Mexico
Albuquerques Best Milkshakes
Mobil travel guide
quality rated
FLAMMABLE
NO SMOKING
DIESEL
ANTIQUE ARCHAEOLOGY
DOWNTOWN
RAINBO BREAD
SLOW
NO ADMITTANCE
AUTHORIZED PERSONNEL ONLY
Dr Pepper
66DINER
1839 224
148 AJR
3699
CAUTION
DO NOT WATCH WELDING ARC
PARKING FOR
66 DINER
ONLY
ALL OTHERS WILL BE POUNDED INTO FLATWARE
NO LOITERING OR SOLICITING ON THIS PROPERTY
The Pile Up
66 DINER
ALBUQUERQUE
ETHYL
DANGER
KEEP OUT
QUALITY CHEKD
PUSH BUTTON FOR WALK SIGNAL
249 550
R 6720
68 604
25 192
591
SC 1652
PENNZOIL
ROAD
CENTRAL AVE.
CLOSED
HISTORIC U.S. 66 ROUTE
Protect Yourself From DEADLY GAS
Phillips
DANGEROUS
ONE WAY
TH LANE
CHILD AT P

June 2026

MAY 2026

					1	2
3	4	5	6	7	8	9
10	11	12	13	14	15	16
17	18	19	20	21	22	23
24/31	25	26	27	28	29	30

JULY 2026

			1	2	3	4
5	6	7	8	9	10	11
12	13	14	15	16	17	18
19	20	21	22	23	24	25
26	27	28	29	30	31	

SUNDAY	MONDAY	TUESDAY	WEDNESDAY	THURSDAY	FRIDAY	SATURDAY
	1 First day of LGBTQ+ Pride Month	2	3	4	5	6
7	8	9	10	11	12	13 Sandia Pueblo Feast Day
14 Flag Day	15	16	17	18	19 Juneteenth	20
21 Father's Day	22	23	24 Ohkay Owingeh Pueblo Feast Day	25	26	27
28	29 Full Moon	30				

Retro signs adorn the exterior of 66 Diner in Albuquerque.
Photograph by Jen Judge.

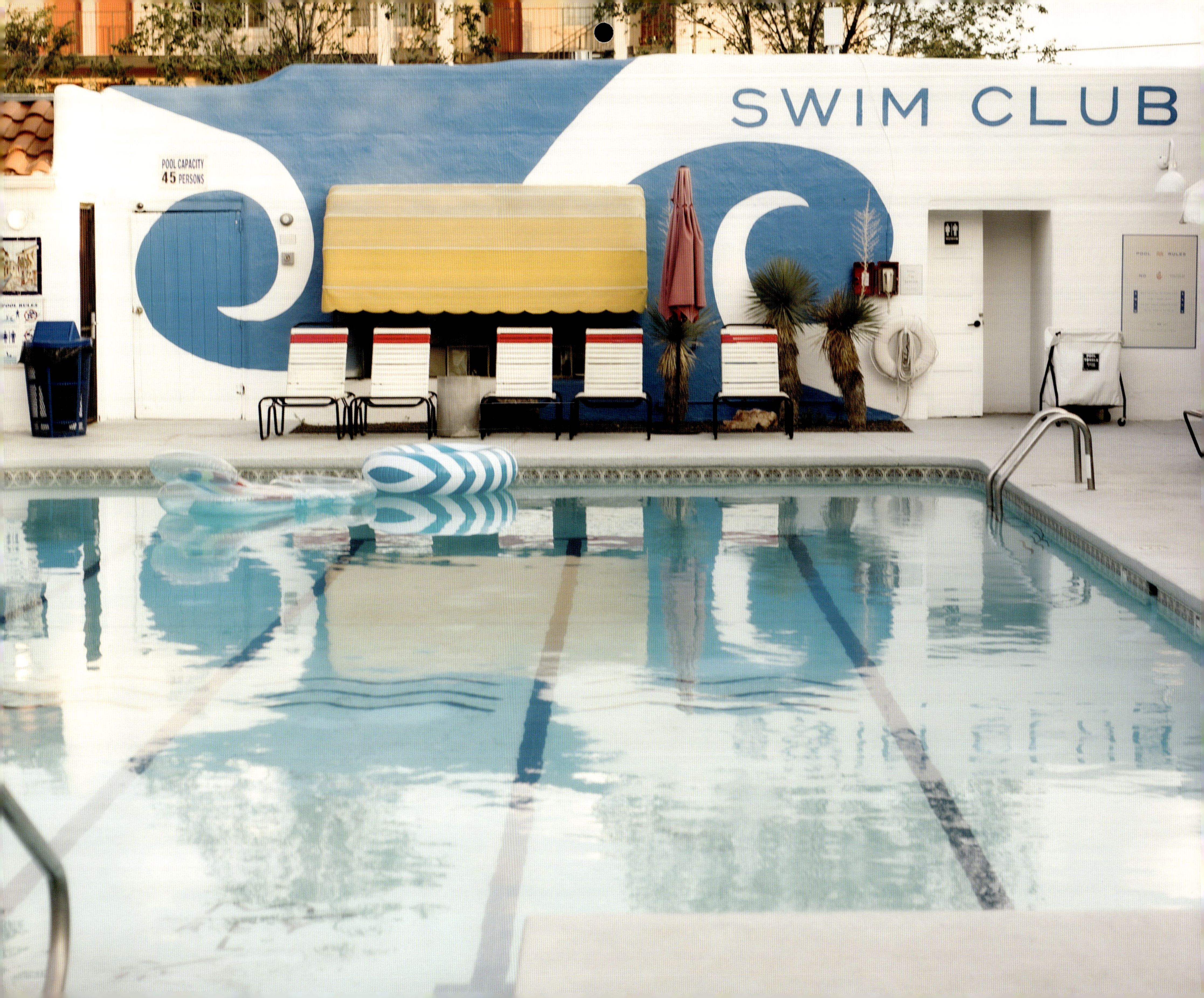
SWIM CLUB
POOL CAPACITY
45 PERSONS

JUNE 2026

	1	2	3	4	5	6
7	8	9	10	11	12	13
14	15	16	17	18	19	20
21	22	23	24	25	26	27
28	29	30				

July 2026

AUGUST 2026

						1
2	3	4	5	6	7	8
9	10	11	12	13	14	15
16	17	18	19	20	21	22
23/30	24/31	25	26	27	28	29

SUNDAY	MONDAY	TUESDAY	WEDNESDAY	THURSDAY	FRIDAY	SATURDAY
			1	2	3	4 Independence Day
5	6	7	8	9	10	11
12	13	14 Cochiti Pueblo Feast Day	15	16	17	18
19	20	21	22	23	24	25
26 Santa Ana Pueblo Feast Day	27	28	29 Full Moon	30	31	

Cool off at El Rey Court hotel's pool in Santa Fe.
Courtesy of El Rey Court/Elizabeth Wells Photography.

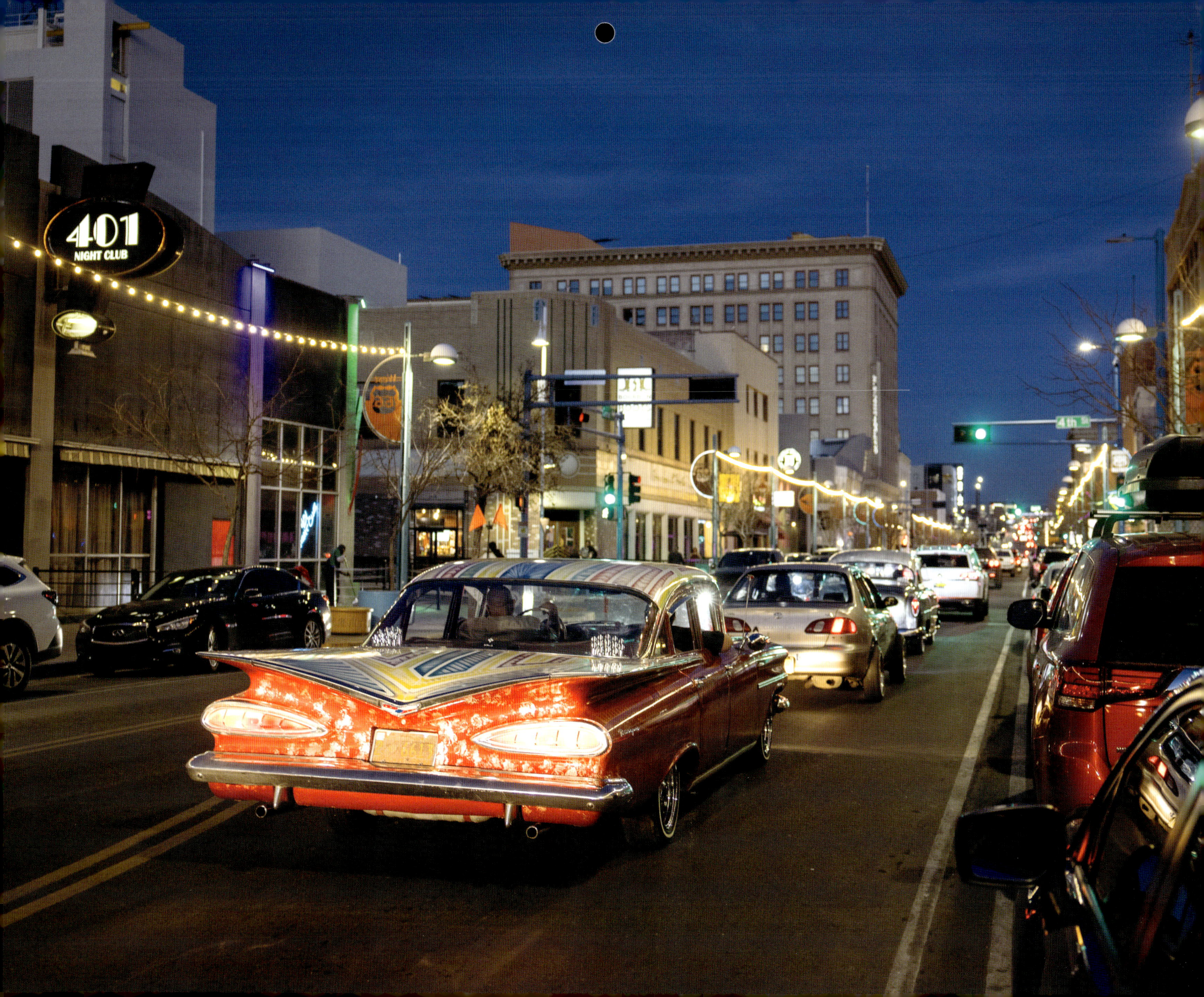
401
NIGHT CLUB
4th

JULY 2026						
			1	2	3	4
5	6	7	8	9	10	11
12	13	14	15	16	17	18
19	20	21	22	23	24	25
26	27	28	29	30	31	

August 2026

SEPTEMBER 2026						
		1	2	3	4	5
6	7	8	9	10	11	12
13	14	15	16	17	18	19
20	21	22	23	24	25	26
27	28	29	30			

SUNDAY	MONDAY	TUESDAY	WEDNESDAY	THURSDAY	FRIDAY	SATURDAY
						1
2 Jemez Pueblo Feast Day	3	4 Santo Domingo Pueblo Feast Day	5	6	7	8
9	10 Picuris Pueblo Feast Day	11	12 Santa Clara Pueblo Feast Day	13	14	15 Zia Pueblo Feast Day
16	17	18	19	20	21	22
23 / 30	24 / 31	25	26	27	28 Isleta Pueblo Feast Day; Full Moon	29

Classic cars still cruise Central Avenue in Albuquerque.
Photograph by Jen Judge.

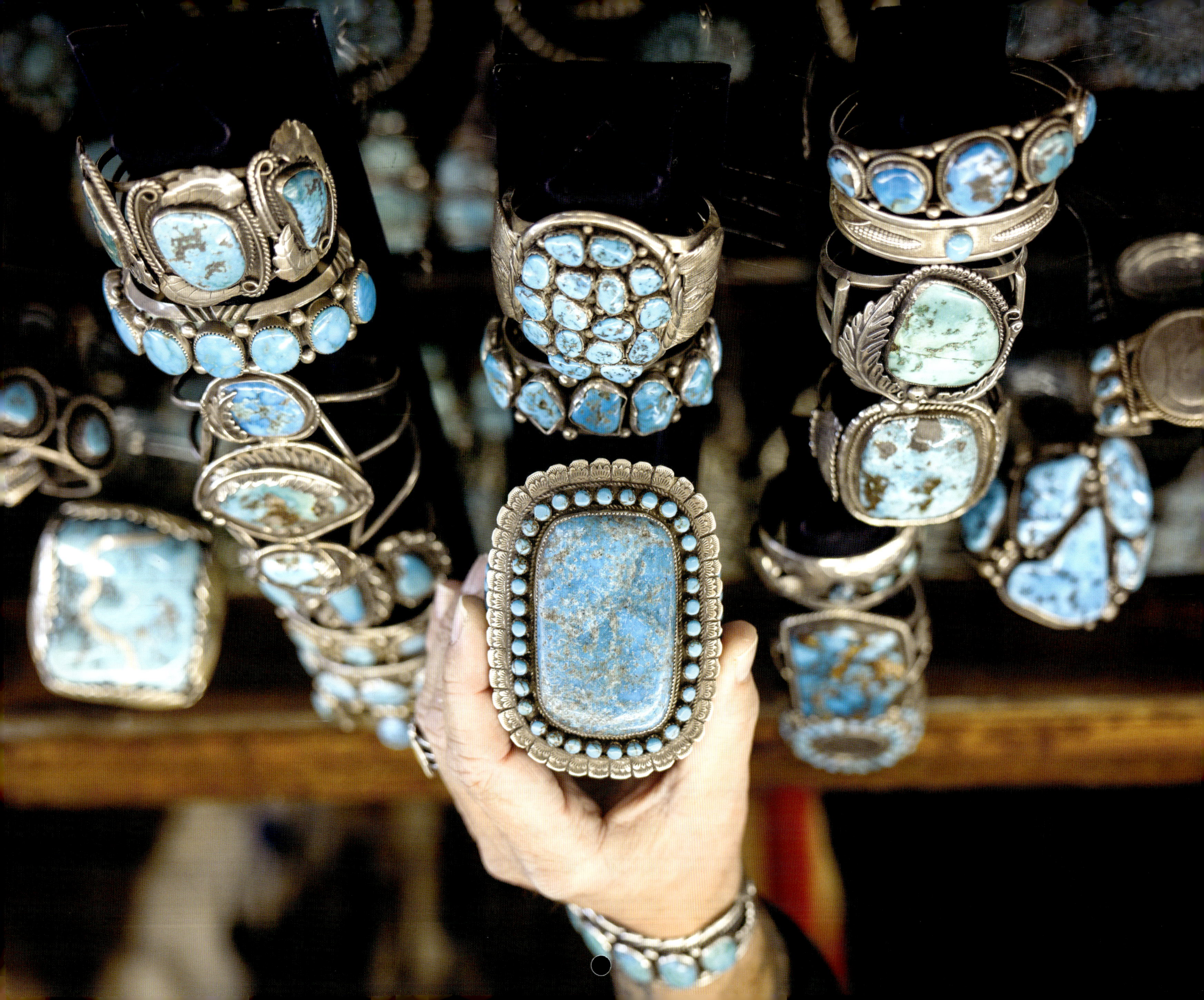

September 2026

AUGUST 2026

						1
2	3	4	5	6	7	8
9	10	11	12	13	14	15
16	17	18	19	20	21	22
23/30	24/31	25	26	27	28	29

OCTOBER 2026

				1	2	3
4	5	6	7	8	9	10
11	12	13	14	15	16	17
18	19	20	21	22	23	24
25	26	27	28	29	30	31

SUNDAY	MONDAY	TUESDAY	WEDNESDAY	THURSDAY	FRIDAY	SATURDAY
		1	2 Acoma Pueblo Feast Day	3	4	5
6	7 Labor Day	8 Laguna Pueblo Feast Day	9	10	11	12 Beginning of Rosh Hashanah
13	14	15 First day of Hispanic Heritage Month	16	17	18	19 Laguna Pueblo Feast Day
20	21 Yom Kippur begins	22	23	24	25 Laguna Pueblo Feast Day	26 Full Moon
27	28	29	30 Taos Pueblo Feast Day			

Richardson Trading Post in Gallup features handcrafted Native turquoise jewelry.
Photograph by Jen Judge.

New Mexico MAGAZINE

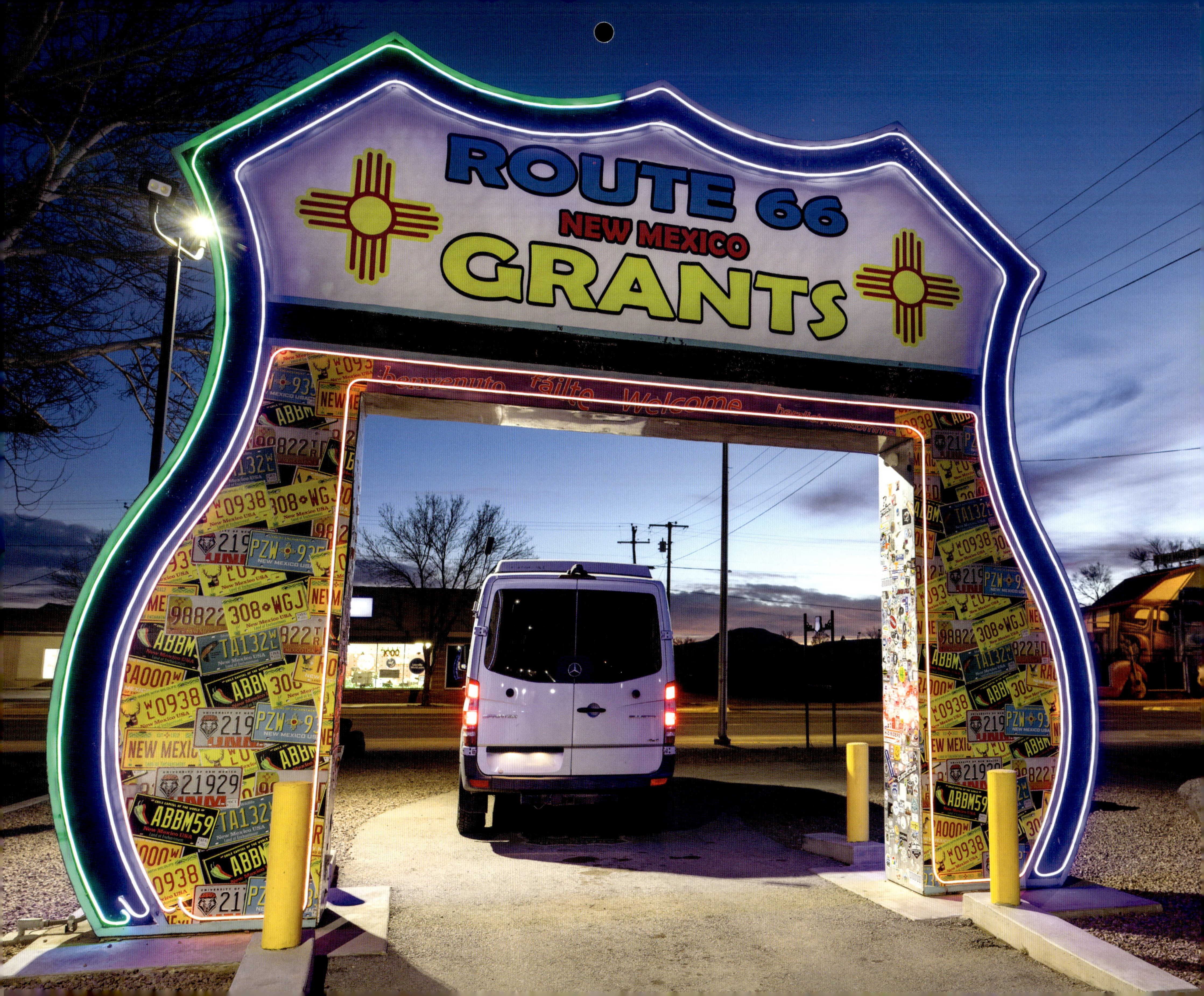
ROUTE 66
NEW MEXICO
GRANTS
benvenuto
fáilte
Welcome

SEPTEMBER 2026

		1	2	3	4	5
6	7	8	9	10	11	12
13	14	15	16	17	18	19
20	21	22	23	24	25	26
27	28	29	30			

October 2026

NOVEMBER 2026

1	2	3	4	5	6	7
8	9	10	11	12	13	14
15	16	17	18	19	20	21
22	23	24	25	26	27	28
29	30					

SUNDAY	MONDAY	TUESDAY	WEDNESDAY	THURSDAY	FRIDAY	SATURDAY
				1	2	3
4 Nambé Pueblo Feast Day	5	6	7	8	9	10
11	12 Indigenous Peoples' Day	13	14	15	16	17 Laguna Pueblo Feast Day
18	19	20	21	22	23	24
25	26 ○ Full Moon	27	28	29	30	31 Halloween

Snap a picture at the Route 66 neon drive-thru arch in Grants.
Photograph by Jen Judge.

New Mexico
MAGAZINE

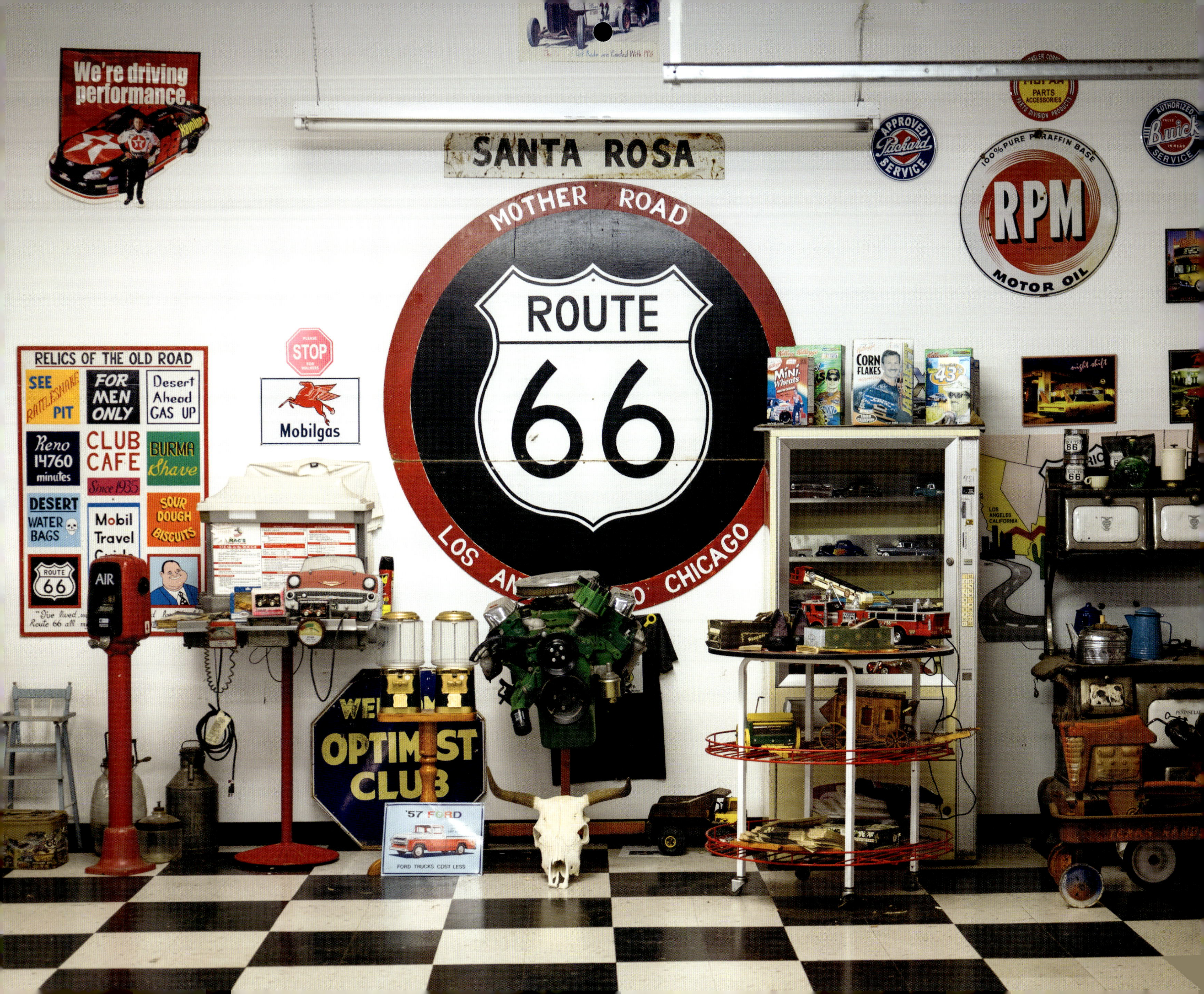

We're driving performance.
SANTA ROSA
MOTHER ROAD
ROUTE 66
LOS
CHICAGO
STOP
Mobilgas
RELICS OF THE OLD ROAD
SEE RATTLESNAKE PIT
FOR MEN ONLY
Desert Ahead GAS UP
Reno 14760 minutes
CLUB CAFE
Since 1935
BURMA Shave
DESERT WATER BAGS
Mobil Travel
SOUR DOUGH BISCUITS
ROUTE 66
AIR
OPTIMIST CLUB
'57 FORD
FORD TRUCKS COST LESS
CORN FLAKES
Mini Wheats
APPROVED Packard SERVICE
AUTHORIZED Buick SERVICE
100% PURE PARAFFIN BASE
RPM
MOTOR OIL
MOPAR PARTS ACCESSORIES

OCTOBER 2026

				1	2	3
4	5	6	7	8	9	10
11	12	13	14	15	16	17
18	19	20	21	22	23	24
25	26	27	28	29	30	31

November 2026

DECEMBER 2026

		1	2	3	4	5
6	7	8	9	10	11	12
13	14	15	16	17	18	19
20	21	22	23	24	25	26
27	28	29	30	31		

SUNDAY	MONDAY	TUESDAY	WEDNESDAY	THURSDAY	FRIDAY	SATURDAY
1	2	3 Election Day	4	5	6	7
8	9	10	11 Route 66 Centennial Veterans Day	12 Jemez Pueblo Feast Day Tesuque Pueblo Feast Day	13	14
15	16	17	18	19	20	21
22	23	24 Full Moon	25	26 Thanksgiving	27 Native American Heritage Day	28
29	30					

The Route 66 Auto Museum in Santa Rosa showcases Mother Road memorabilia.
Photograph by Jen Judge.

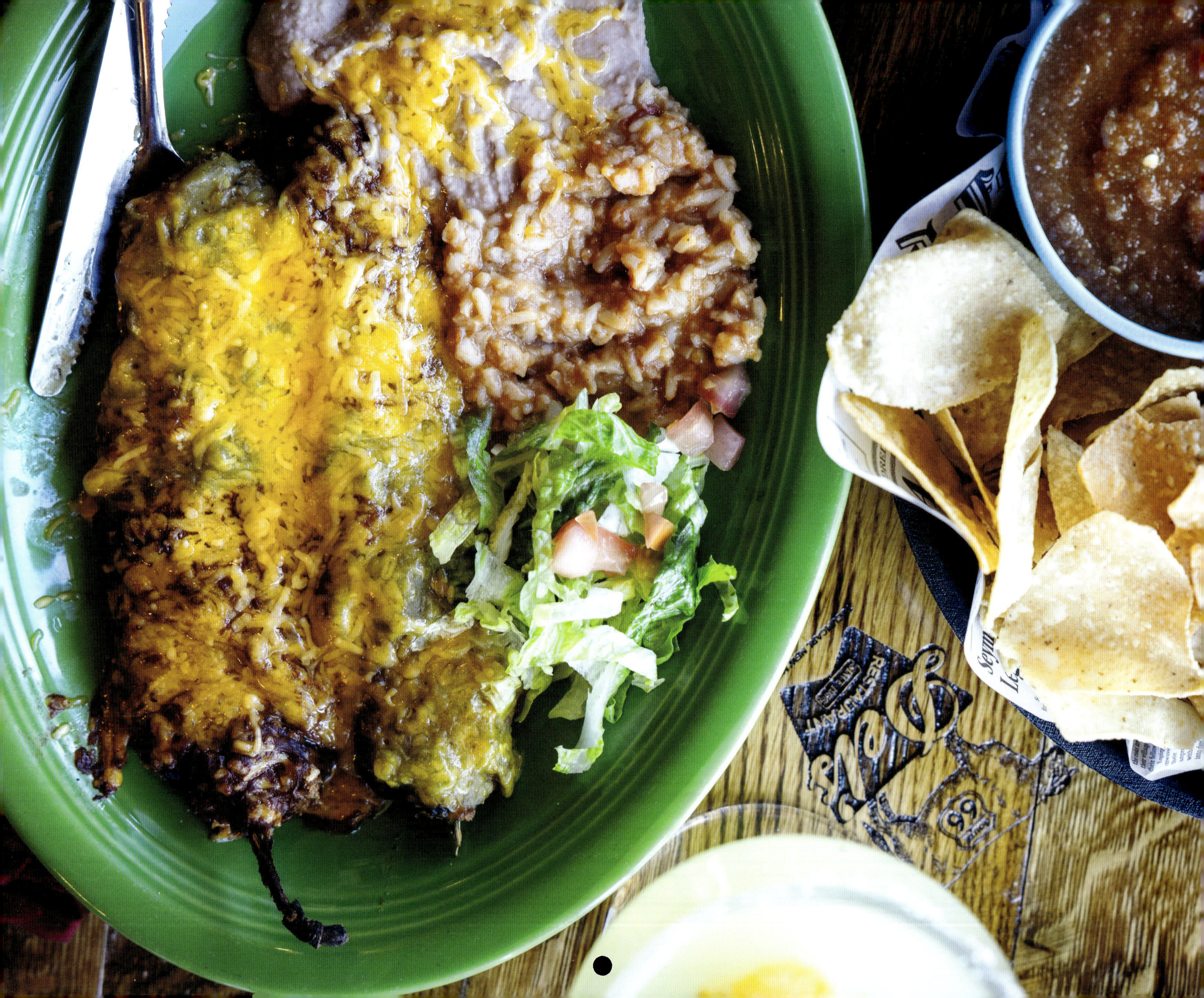
RESTAURANT
66